SharePoint Server 2010 Trivia

{33 Random Quick Tips}

STEVEN MANN

SharePoint 2010 Trivia {33 Random Quick Tips}

About the Author

Steve Mann was born and raised in Philadelphia, Pennsylvania, where he still resides. He is Enterprise Applications Engineer for Morgan Lewis and has more than 16 years of professional experience. Steve was previously a Principal Architect for RDA Corporation where he worked for over 13 years. He has authored and co-authored several books related to the subject of SharePoint Server 2010.

For the past 7 years, he has primarily focused on collaboration and business intelligence solutions using Microsoft technologies. Steve managed the internal BI Practice Group at RDA for several years. He was also heavily involved within RDA's Collaboration/Search Practice Group.

Steve's blog site can be found at: www.SteveTheManMann.com

Introduction

This book is intended to point out things to notice, be aware of, and/or look out for within the SharePoint Server 2010 product (and supporting products) from Microsoft. Originally the concept was to be funny and point out solutions to frustrations but in order to be able to use the screenshots and comply with Microsoft's policies, I decided not to write anything that could be interpreted as disparaging, defamatory, or libelous.

As you work with SharePoint 2010 (or SharePoint in general), there are several learning curves involved. I say "several" since there are various aspects of SharePoint – development, administration, end-user, etc.

Some curves are obviously steeper than others and vary by the individual person. Nonetheless we all run, have run, or will run into the same problems or come across items that may seem annoying at first.

Therefore, this book can be used as a quick hit learning tool to help straighten the curves, gain clarification on items, and/or possibly understand something before you run into issues.

Enjoy!

#1

Site Actions on Left

The first thing you will notice in SharePoint Server 2010 (other than the layout, colors, styles, etc.) is that the Site Actions menu is now on the left of the screen.

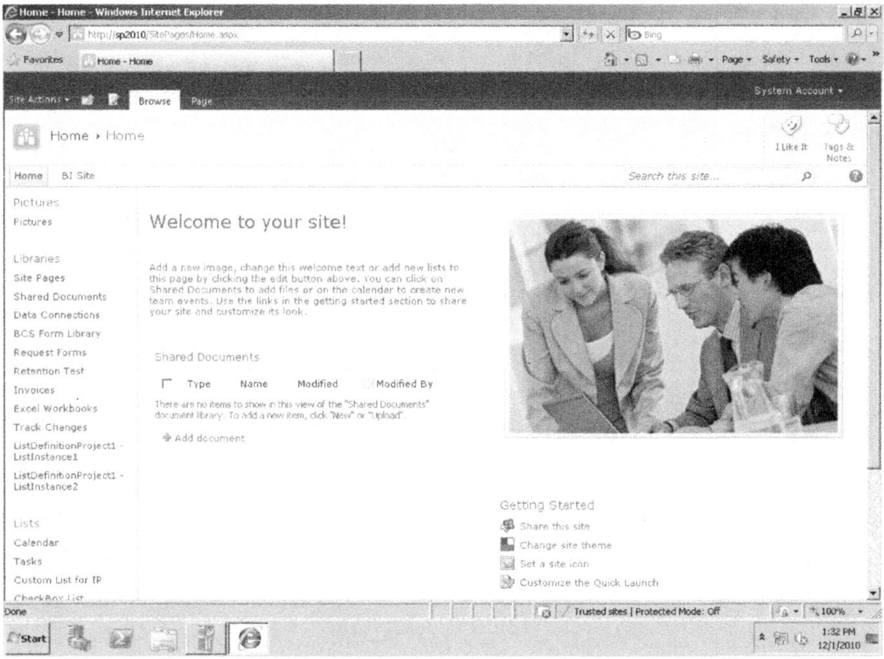

If you have been using MOSS 2007 for, let's say, the last three-four years, you are used to the Site Actions menu being on the right. It only takes a few days to adjust to this modification.

#2 Site Actions in Site Settings

Now that you have found the Site Actions menu, select Site Settings. Wow, there are more Site Actions.

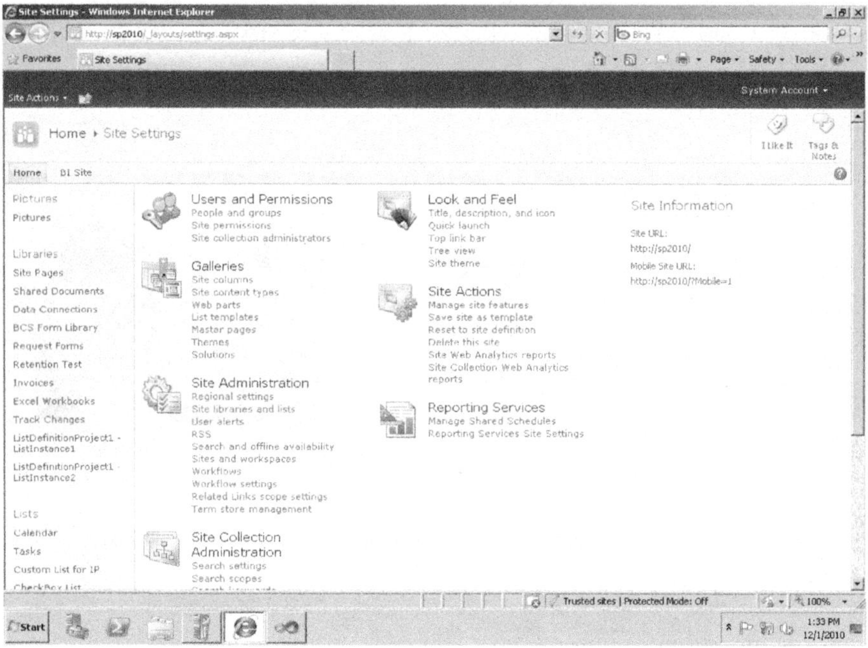

The menu is called Site Actions but there is a section in Site Settings called Site Actions. When speaking to users or developers, make sure you clarify which Site Actions you are referring.

#3 Site Collection Features

Manage site features is the first option under Site Actions. This is where you manage features that can be activated at the site level. For features at the site collection level, use the link under the Site Collection Administration section.

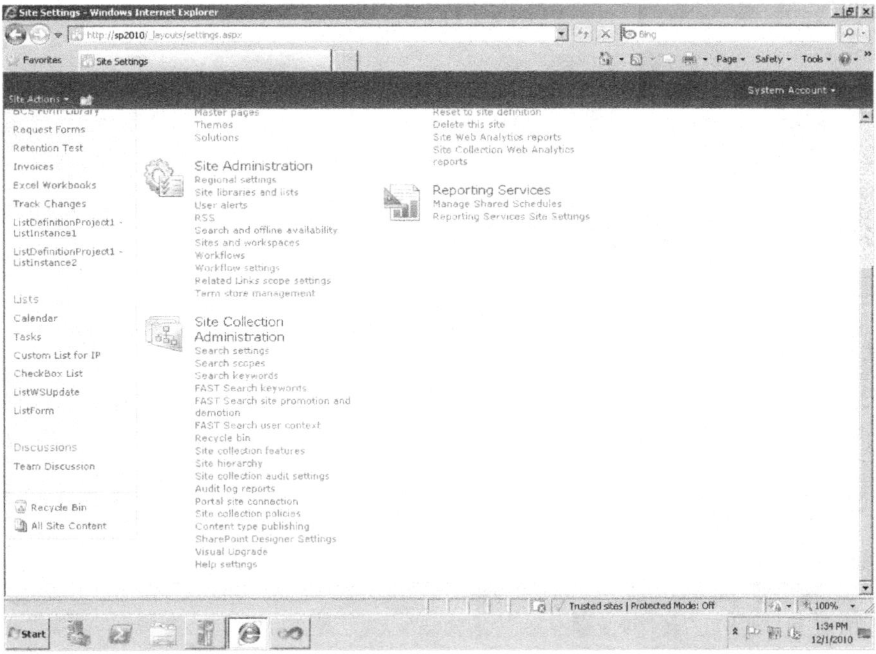

That link just says Site collection features. There is no "Manage" in front of that one – just something to notice and be aware. You can use that screen to Activate or Deactivate features at the site collection level.

#4 Feature Scope

Speaking of Site Features and Site Collection Features, when creating these things in Visual Studio (or by hand I guess – yes that's possible and I think I've done it at least once before in MOSS 2007), the feature target is determined by the scope.

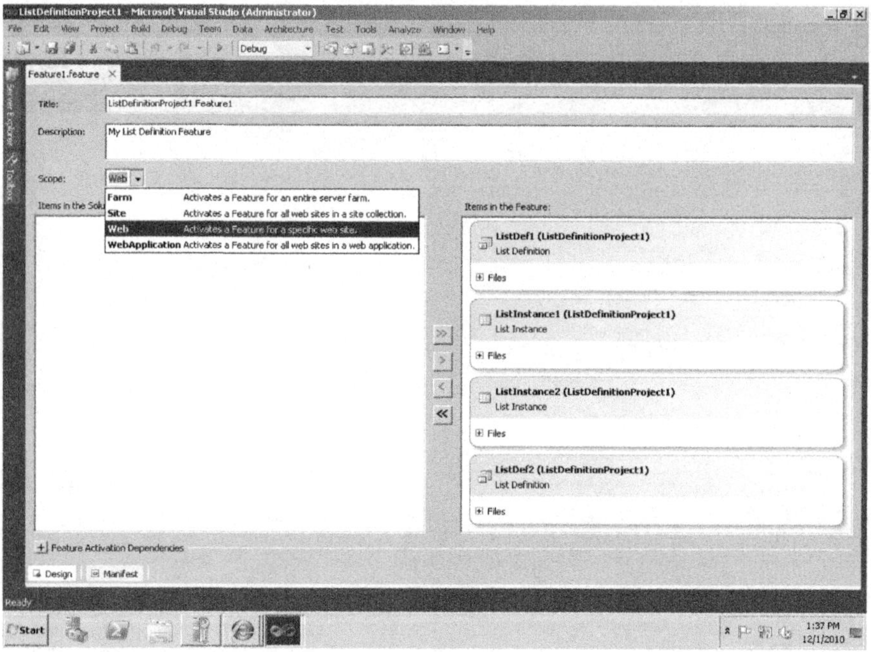

Ironically, the Site scope is not for a site feature but a site collection feature. A feature for a site is scoped as Web. This stems from the underlying object model where SPSite is a site collection and SPWeb is a site. Confused yet? Luckily there is an explanation in the drop-down box in Visual Studio 2010.

#5 Timer Jobs - Run Now

When you look at the Timer Job defimition, there is a button to run the job now.

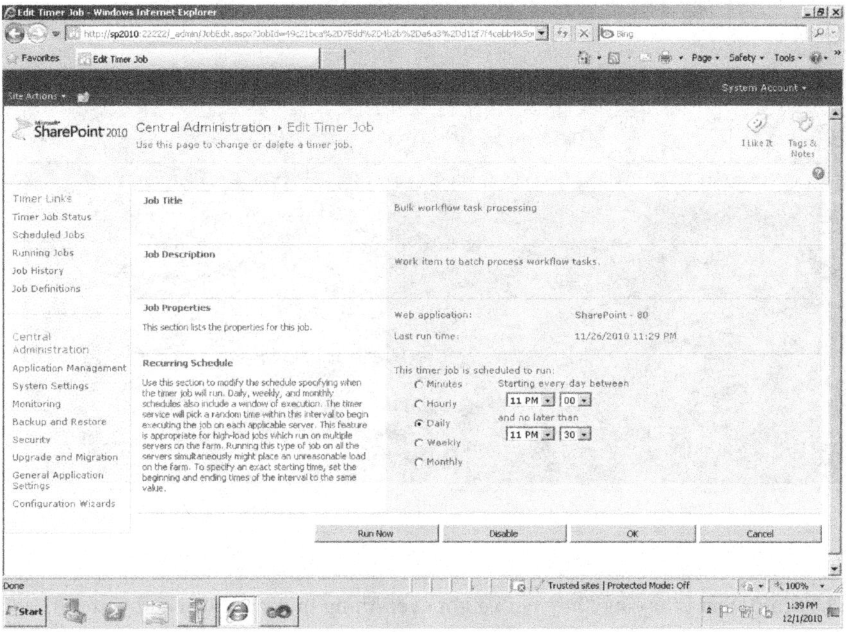

That doesn't actually make the job run right away. It means that it will be scheduled to run right away but the timer service still needs to kick it off. So it is not exactly instant.

#6 ExecAdmSvcJobs

In MOSS 2007, if there was something in the queue that needed to be run, you could force it to run sooner by using STSADM with the ExecAdmSvcJobs operation. If you try to force jobs by using that operation, you now get a nice message.

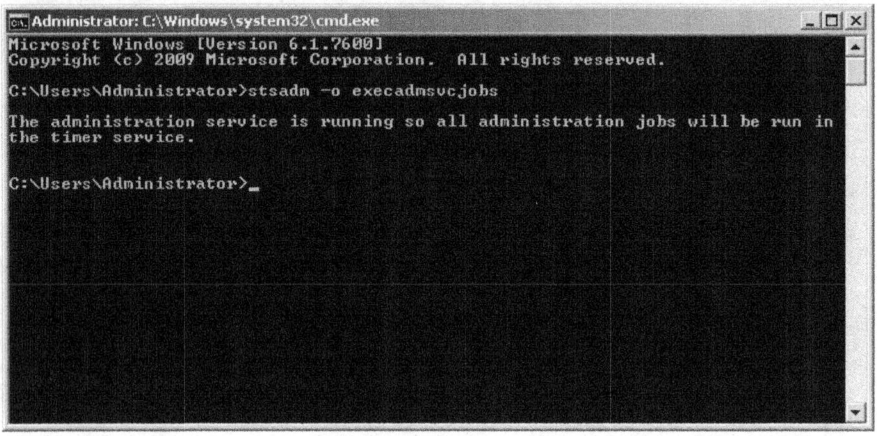

So basically that is saying "hey we've got everything under control and you will be seated as soon as possible". There is no more bypassing the system – the jobs will run when they run.

#7

Debugging Timer Job Code

If you decide to create your own timer job (which is actually easier than it sounds), you may need to debug the code or other custom assembly code that the job may execute. (You debug timer job code by attaching to the OWSTIMER process). Sometimes you may come across some strange logic behavior.

Everytime you update the code you must restart the timer service. Otherwise the job will execute the original code since it caches the assemblies. I have seen debugging behavior when the code doesn't match the assembly but in some cases the trace actually looks like the logic isn't being evaluated or processed correctly.

#8

Scheduling Timer Jobs

You can schedule timer jobs to run between certain times – just like scheduling cable service. In the example below, it will run anytime between 2am and 6am in the morning.

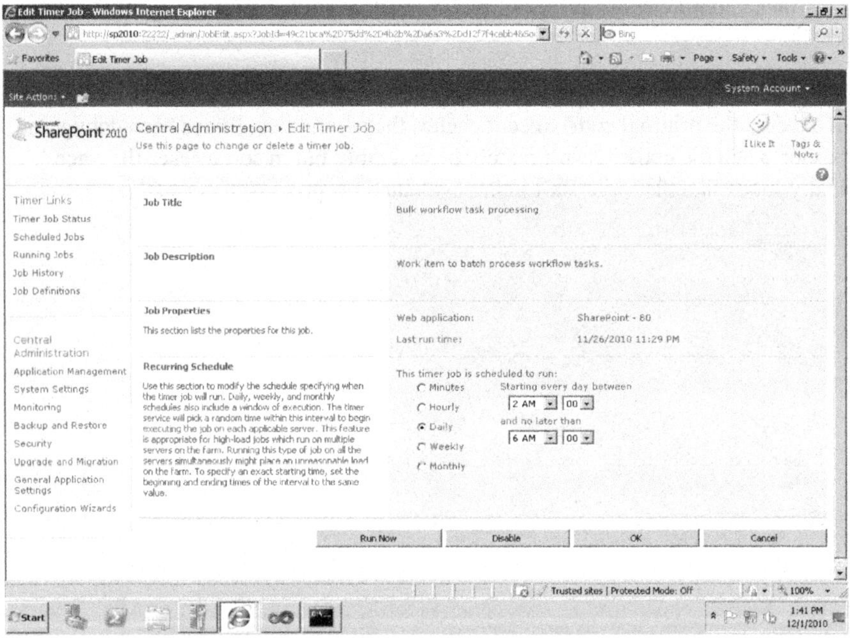

This is good since SharePoint will manage various jobs that need to run overnight within the same time frames and insure that nothing steps on each other.

#9 List Definition Warning

When you create a List Definition for SharePoint in Visual Studio 2010, you get a warning (shown as a comment) in the Elements.xml not to change the name as the folder needs to be the same name.

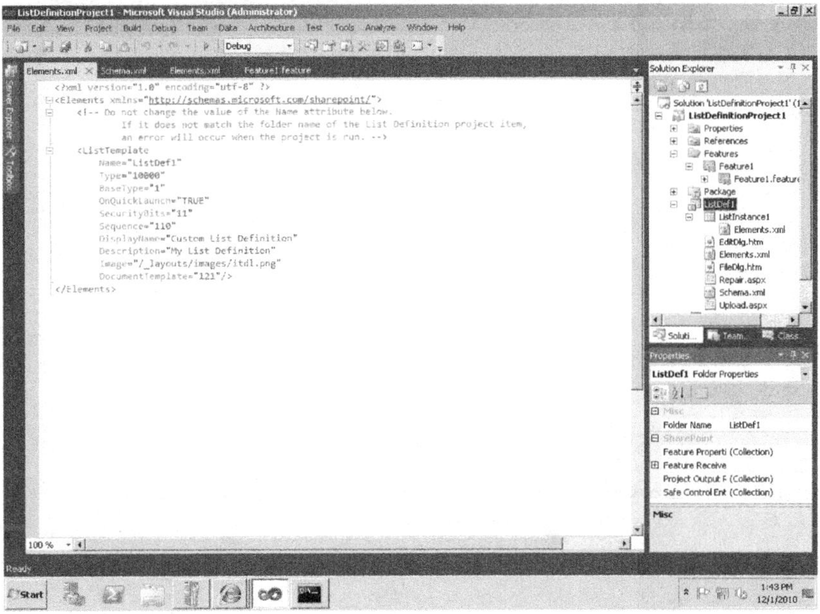

You can change the the Name as long as you change the folder name to match. In fact, if youchange the folder name first, it will update the name in the Elements.xml automatically!

#10 Unique List Definition

Everytime you create a List Definition and deploy it, that list definition is added to available types when creating a new list or library from within SharePoint.

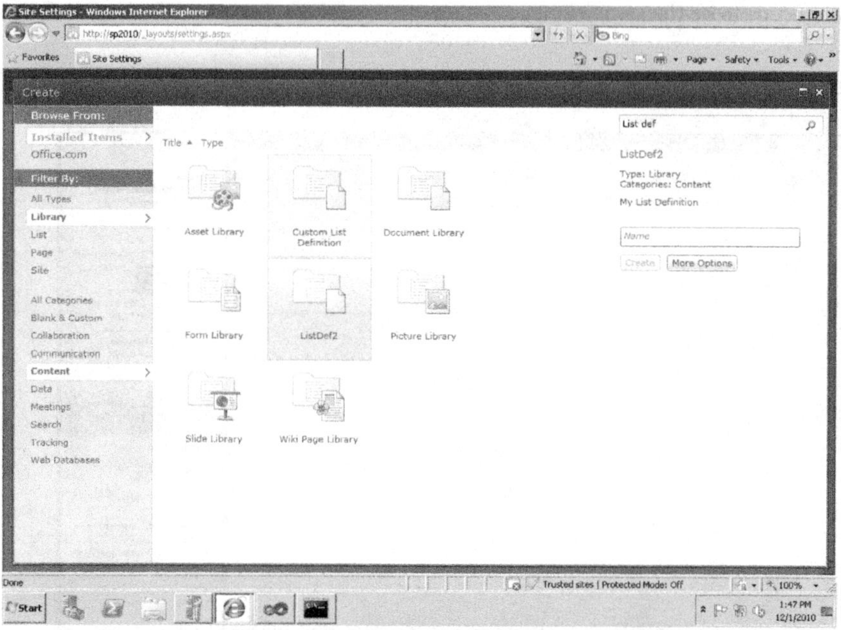

Many times, you only need to create an instance of a list or library once. So you don't need every type showing up in the users' create dialogs. This can easily be fixed by placing a property within the ListTemplate tag of the List Definition Elements.xml.The property is called Unique and setting that to "TRUE" will only use that list definition once – so make sure you are creating a List Instance as part of the List Definition project.

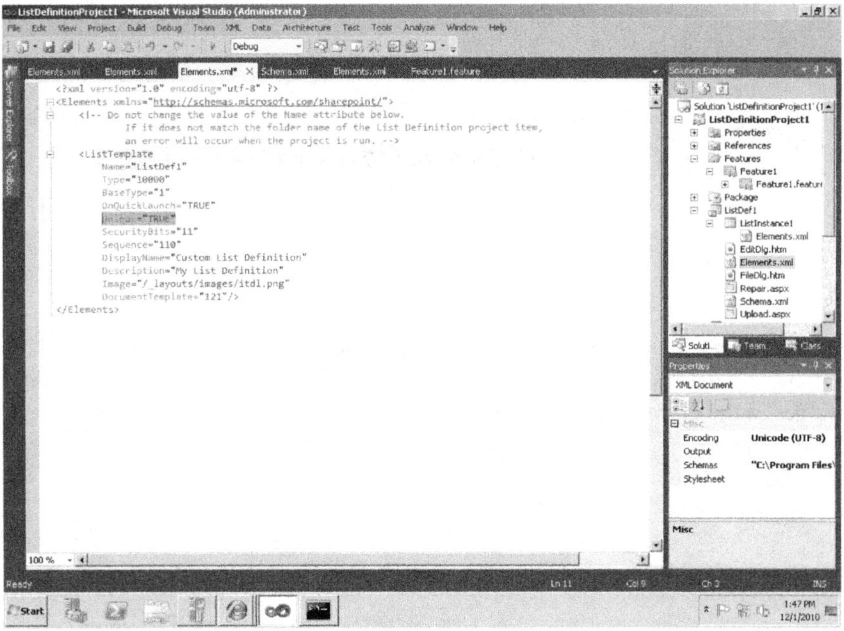
ListDefinitionProject1 - Microsoft Visual Studio (Administrator)
File Edit View Project Build Debug Team XML Data Architecture Test Tools Analyze Window Help
Elements.xml Elements.xml Elements.xml* Schema.xml Elements.xml Feature1.feature
<?xml version="1.0" encoding="utf-8" ?>
<Elements xmlns="http://schemas.microsoft.com/sharepoint/">
<!-- Do not change the value of the Name attribute below.
If it does not match the folder name of the List Definition project item,
an error will occur when the project is run. -->
<ListTemplate
Name="ListDef1"
Type="10000"
BaseType="1"
OnQuickLaunch="TRUE"
Unique="TRUE"
SecurityBits="11"
Sequence="110"
DisplayName="Custom List Definition"
Description="My List Definition"
Image="/_layouts/images/itdl.png"
DocumentTemplate="121"/>
</Elements>
Solution Explorer
Solution 'ListDefinitionProject1'
ListDefinitionProject1
Properties
References
Features
Feature1
Package
ListDef1
ListInstance1
Elements.xml
EditDlg.htm
Elements.xml
FileDlg.htm
Repair.aspx
Schema.xml
Upload.aspx
Properties
XML Document
Encoding
Unicode (UTF-8)
Output
Schemas
Stylesheet
Misc
Ready
Ln 11
Col 9
Ch 3
INS
Start
1:47 PM
12/1/2010

#11 List Definition Schema Tags

If you investigate the Schema.XML file in a List Definition, you'll notice that all of the Views are defined in there. This is good stuff as you can modify fields and add new ones in the views so you don't have to manually do that after the list instance is created.

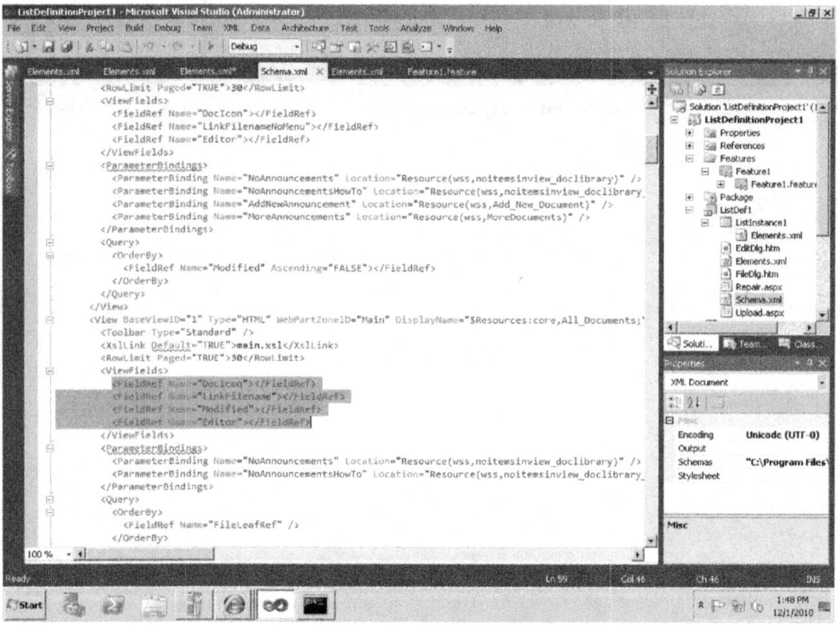

But for some reason, the ViewFields FieldRefs are the only tags that are not self terminated. Notice the </FieldRef>? You can add more fields to your view by copying the field tags from content types (which appear at the top of the Schema.XML) that are self terminated, and paste them here. If the </FieldRef> end tags cramp your style then simply remove them and then add the slash "/" at the end of the <FieldRef> tag.

#12 Default View In List Def Schema

While you are in the Schema.XML and investigating the view definitions, notice the BaseViewID. The main or default view (e.g. All Documents, All Items) is actually BaseViewID="1" although there is a BaseView with an ID of "0".

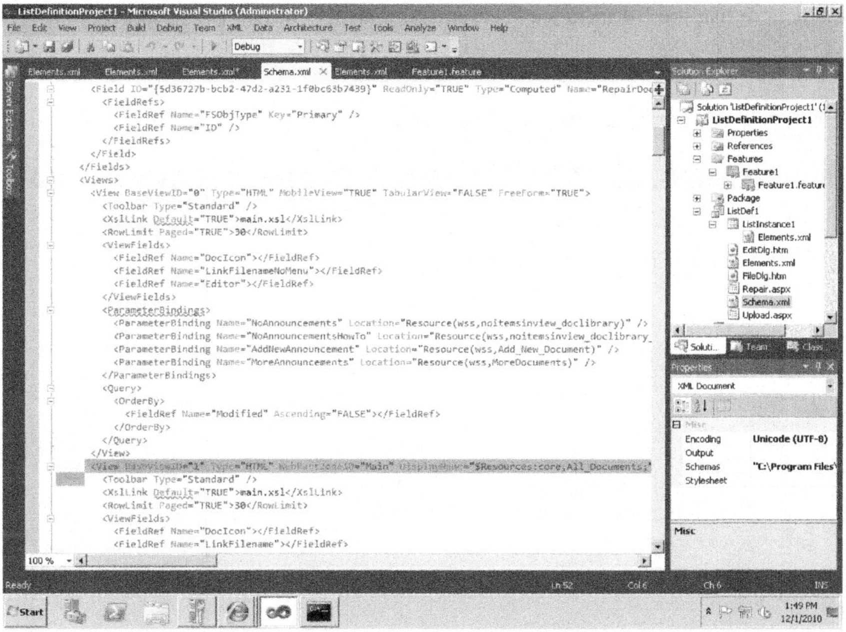

#13 List Instance URL

Even if you are generating document libraries, it is still a list instance. That's because a document library is a type of list. Almost everything in SharePoint is a list whether it appears that way or not.

However, even though you may specify a content type that is a document library and not a custom list, the list instance Elements.xml always has a "Lists/" prefix in the URL.

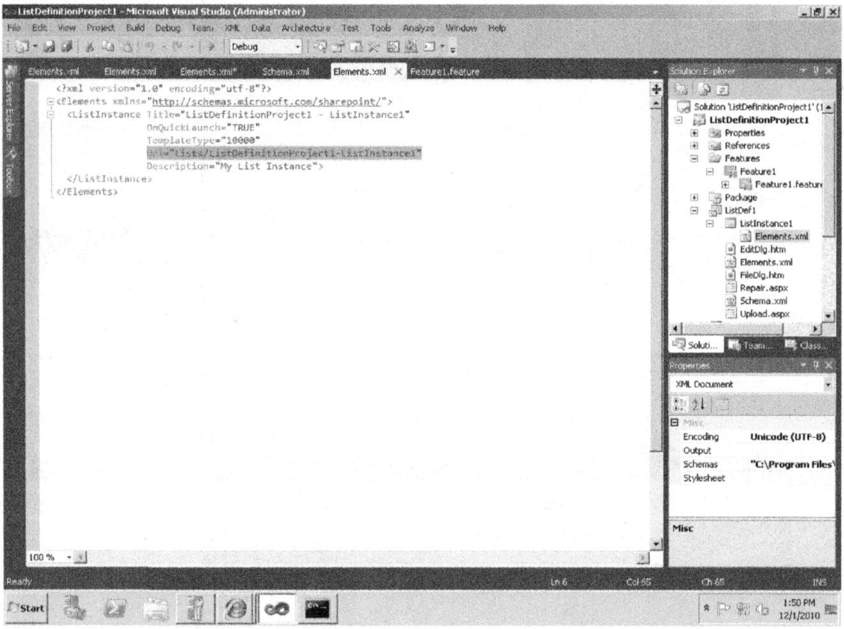

So if you want it to be a Library and not a List, you need to remove the "Lists/" prefix from the URL. This will generate the instance on the root of the site and it will appear under the Libraries quick launch grouping.

#14 Picture Library

Speaking of lists and libraries, have you seen the Picture Library in SharePoint 2010? The Picture Library in SharePoint 2010 is similiar to the Picture Library from MOSS 2007.

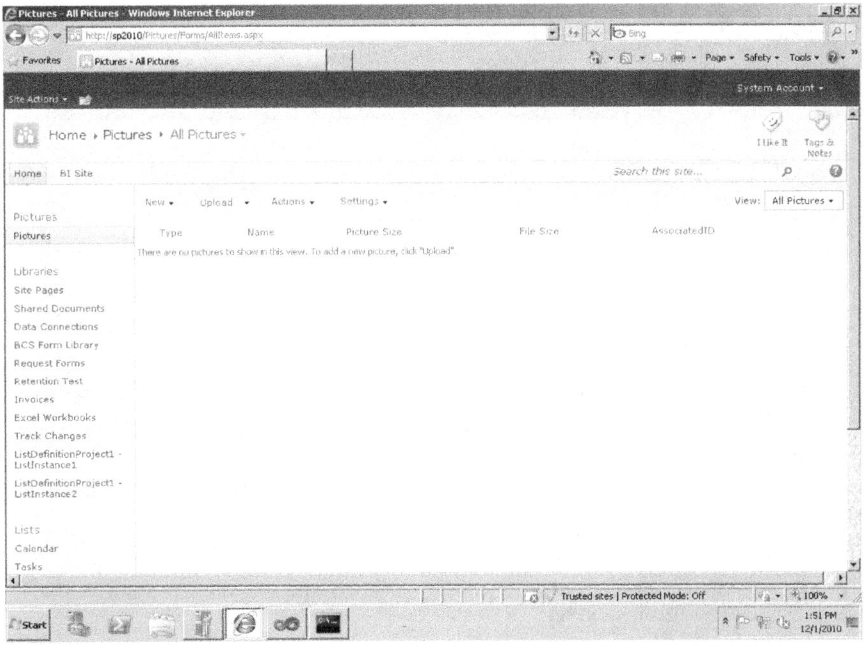

There is no ribbon interface for this type of library. There is a top menu bar just like in MOSS 2007. You won't be able to create a custom form interface for it (ala InfoPath) either.

#15 Manage Service Applications

The Manage Service Applications page from within Central Administration provides a listing of the available service applications running on the farm. Among configuring each service application through their own set of configuration and settings screens, there are also properties, permissions, and other actions that may be taken.

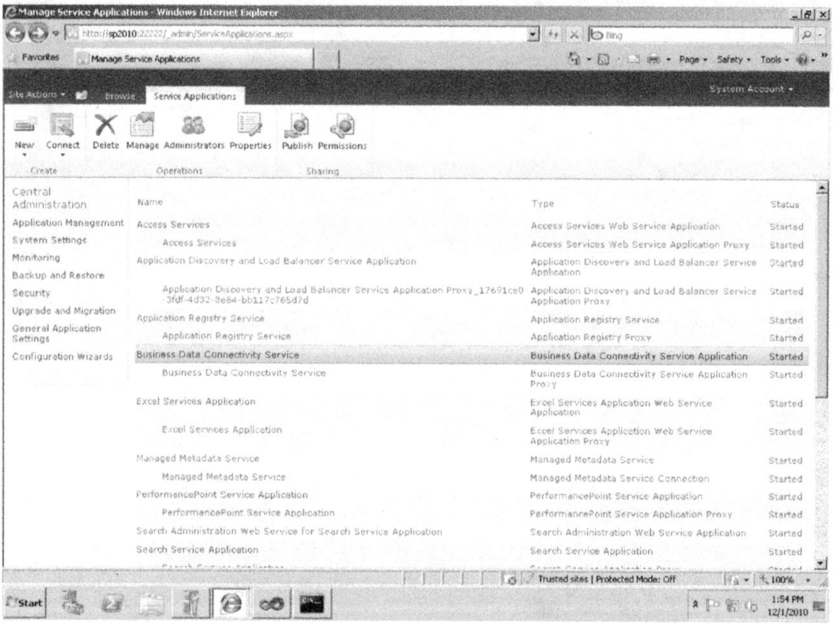

These additional actions appear on the ribbon when a service application is selected. However, since the user tendency is to click on the name (which is actually a link to the configuration pages) , it is easy to forget that there are settings at this main level. The service application gets selected but then navigation is passed to the service application's management page.

#16 Trusted Locations

You don't have to worry about where you can store Excel Services content or PerformancePoint content because by default the entire SharePoint site is trusted.

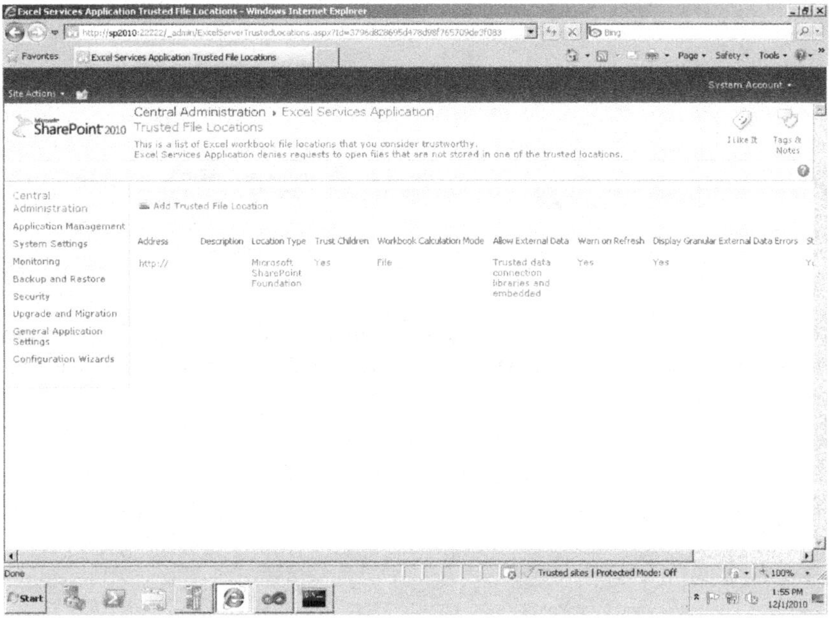

Although, you won't get too far with the Excel Services using data connections because there are no trusted data connection locations setup. However, within PerformancePoint Services, All SharePoint locations are trusted to contain data sources.

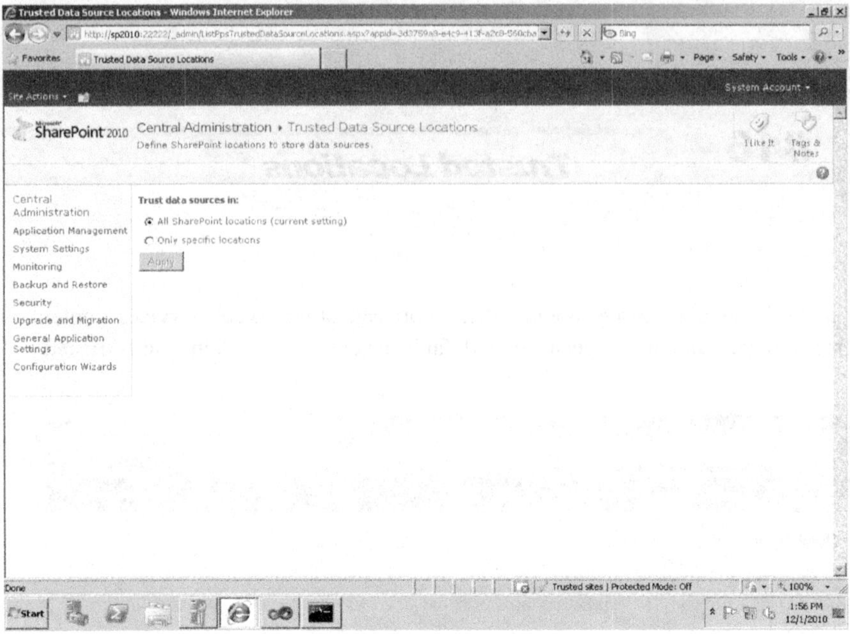

This has pros and cons but at least you know where to configure some of the security around these service applications which can access (possibly sensitive) external data.

#17 Content Deployment – Paths & Jobs

When you setup the Content Deployment Paths and Jobs from within Central Administration (under General Application Settings), you can't setup a New Job until there is a path that exists.

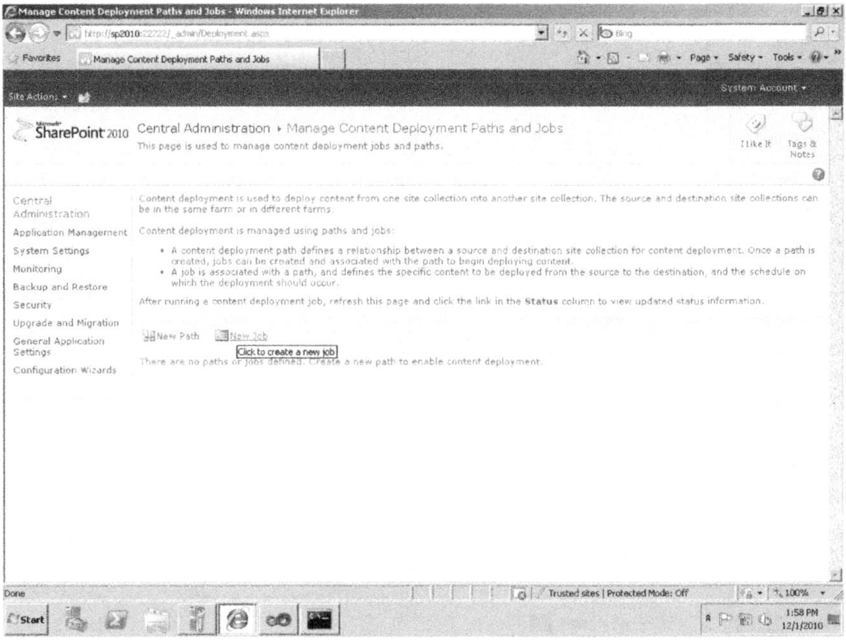

The New Job link is disabled and greyed out however if you hover over it, the underline appears as if it were an active hyperlink and the tooltip appears saying"Click to create a new job". I was caught off guard at one point since I wasn't paying attention. You need to create a New Path first.

#18 Content Deployment – New Path

So you decide to create a new path for Content Deployment.You won't get too far if you are using the same Central Admin site and haven't configured Content Deployment first.

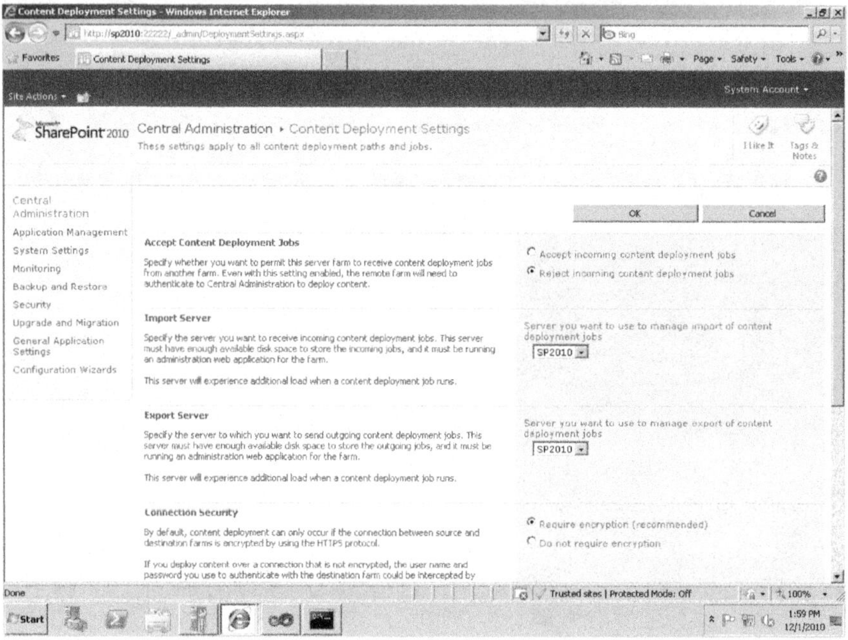

By default, the Content Deployment setting is to Reject incoming content deployment jobs. So before you can create any paths or jobs, you must first change the Central Admin site to Accept incoming content deployment jobs.

#19 Site Directory

There is no such thing as a Site Directory in SharePoint 2010 - it is all gone. The settings in SharePoint 2010 are simply for backwards compatibility purposes.

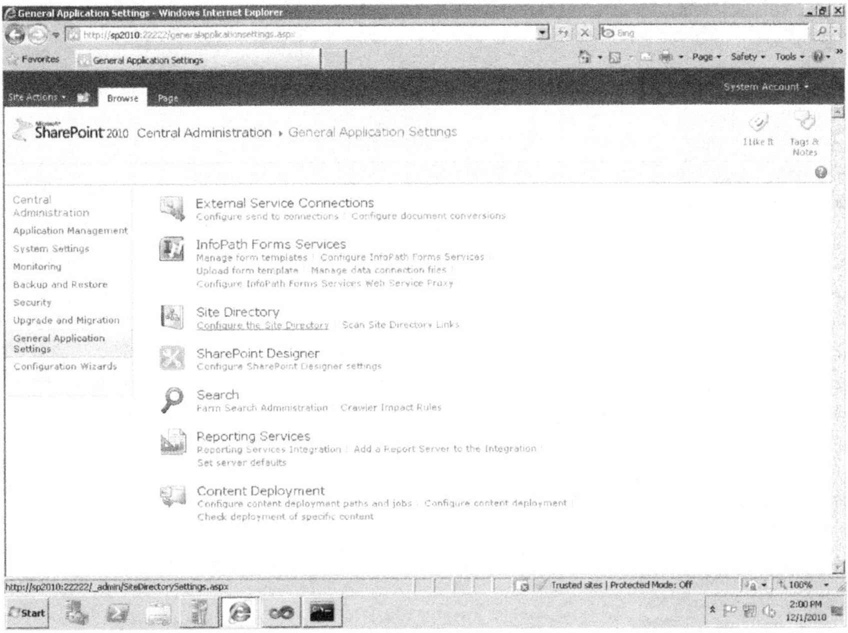

#20 Repair Automatically

Some of the Health Analyzer report entries can be repaired automatically. This is a setting in the Health Analyzer rule item but also a button in the top ribbon of a report item dialog.

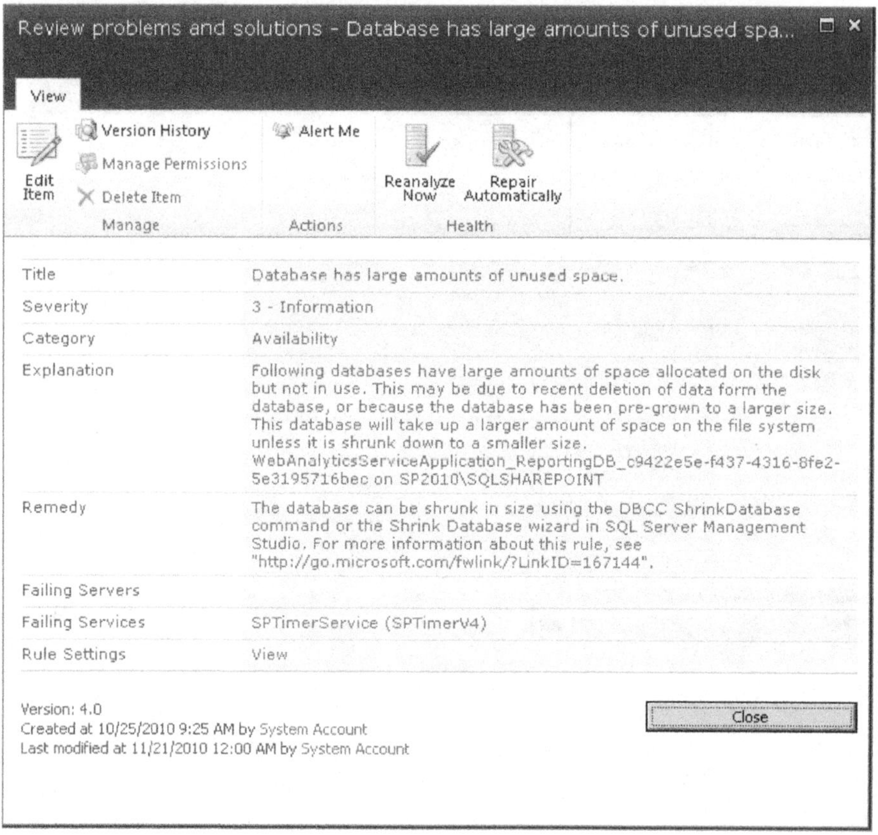

A common informational report item is the fact that one or more databases can be shrunk as there are large amounts of unused space. Pretty easy to resolve and even SharePoint knows how to fix the problem.

Therefore, click Repair Automatically. That just makes the button disabled and you have no idea what happened. The Reanalyze Now button becames enabled. Click that button and that gets disabled without knowing what happened either.

After a few refreshes of the Health Analyzer reports, SharePoint indeed fixes the problem and shrinks the databases. It just takes some time (as it is on a timer job) but eventually it is resolved.

#21 Upgrade Required/Recommended

Occasionally there will be Health Analyzer report items talking about an upgrade is required or recommended.

The item details makes you think that there are updates to be applied or something of that sort. These messages appear when version numbers are out-of-sync. After applying hot-fixes (cumulative updates) you need to run the SharePoint Products Configuration Wizard which can be found in the Start menu under Microsoft SharePoint.

The report item details may confuse you with mentioning PSCONFIG or PSCONFIGUI. These are just fancy technical terms for the SharePoint Products Configuration Wizard (as those are the names of the underlying executables). Simply run the wizard and everything should be back in sync. However, I have seen these Health Analzer items appear when nothing was updated at all and the SharePoint Products Configuration Wizard had been run the week before.

#22 Tags – Private Text

Now you can tag sites and locations within SharePoint. Clicking on the I Like It button simply adds a "I like it" tag.

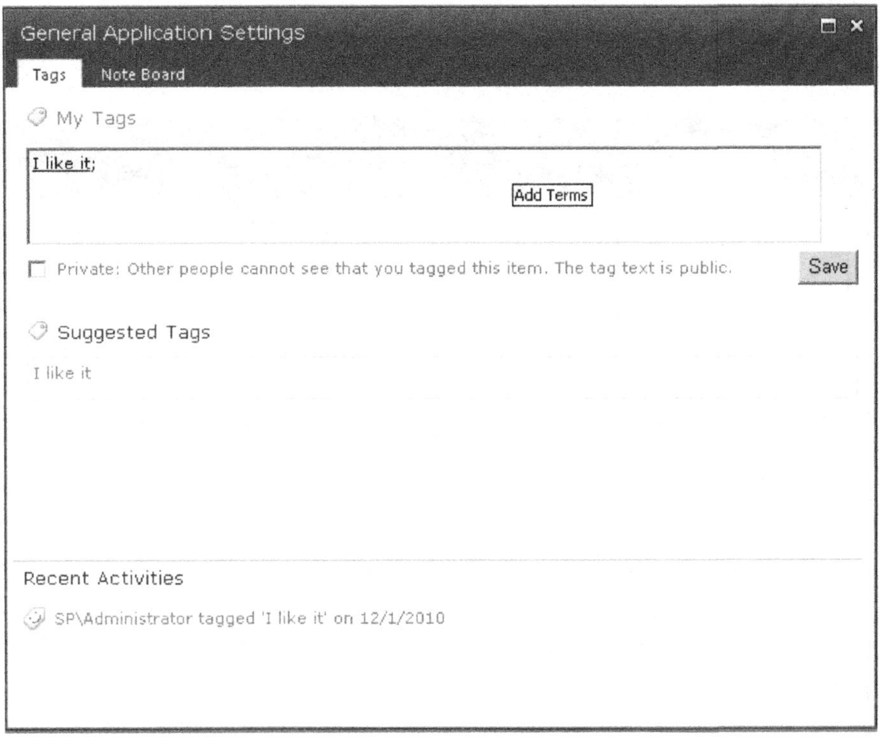

When reviewing your tags under a specific site, there is a Private check box. Essentially if you want the tags to be private you check thre check box. "The tag text is public." is just extra information explaining that if the Private check box is not checked, the tags are public.

#23 Note Board

While you are reviewing the tags, you can also switch to the Note Board tab within that dialog. Here you can add notes or comments about the site or SharePoint location. The notes will appear in your My Site if you have personalization sites configured.

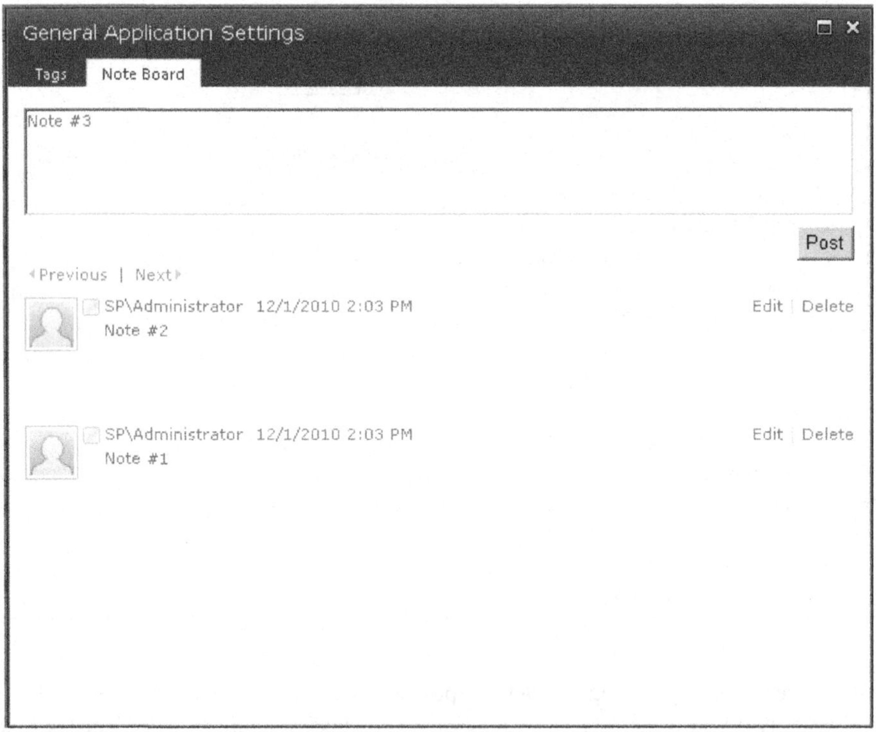

You can use the Previous and Next links once there are "pages" of notes. However, initially they appear but are disabled.

#24 Internet Explorer – 64-bit

If you accidentally run the 64-bit version of Internet Explorer you may get prompted to Install Microsoft® Silverlight:

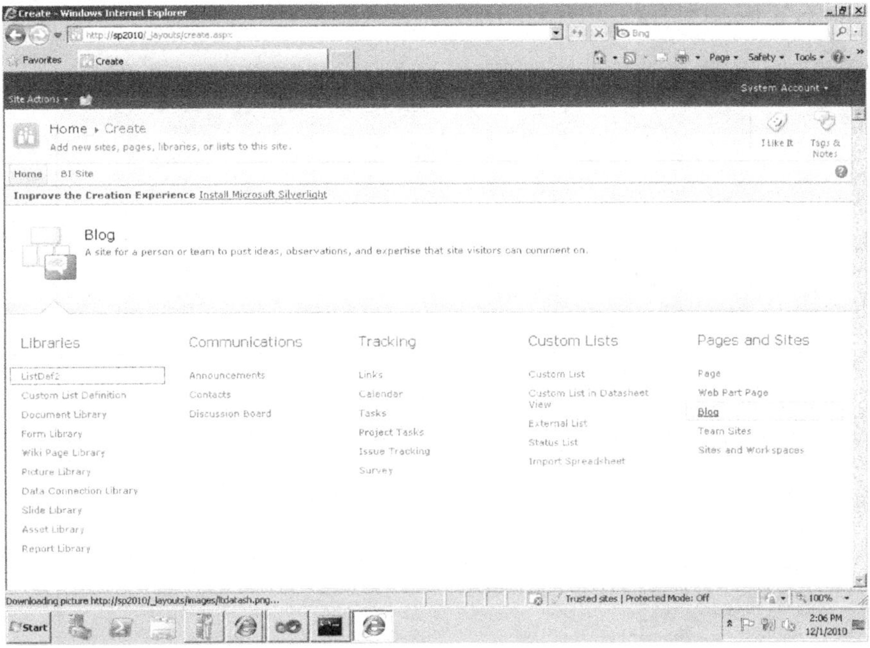

However, when you go to install Silverlight, you are taken to a Microsoft® page that explains that Silverlight cannot be used in browsers running in 64 bit. At least you get the old Create page in this mode and hovering over the items does present a nice detail display.

#25 New Page

If you just select New Page from the Site Actions menu within a team site or site running the Wiki feature, you have no control of what that page is or where it lives. You are forced to create a new page in the Site Pages library and the only option is the name.

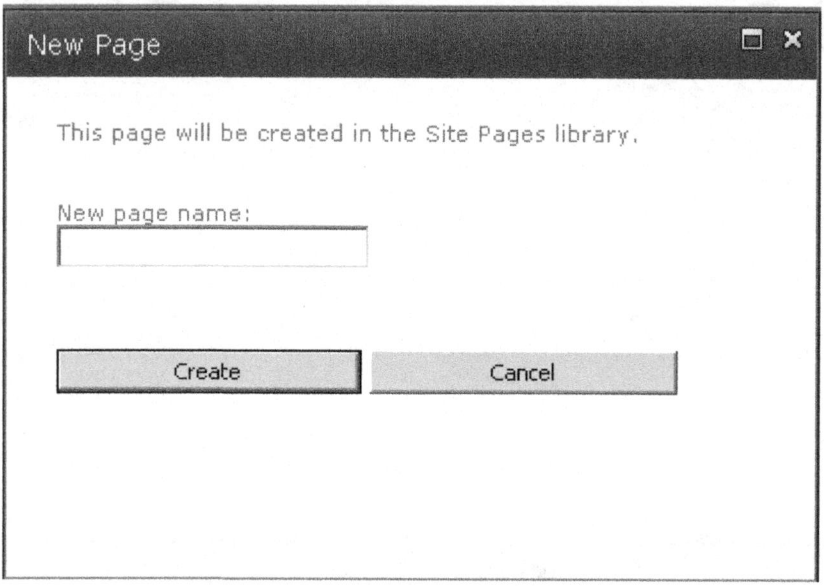

If you use More Options from the Site Actions menu instead, you can actually select what kind of page (e.g. Web Part Page) you wish to create. Once the type of page is selected, you can then select the layout of the page and you can choose where the page will be created.

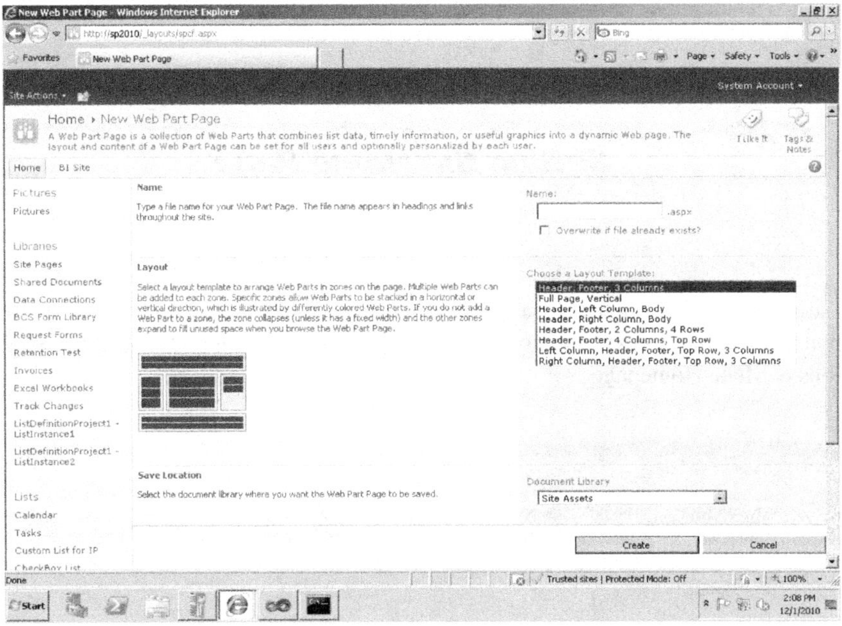

New Web Part Page - Windows Internet Explorer
http://sp2010/_layouts/spcf.aspx
Favorites
New Web Part Page
Page
Safety
Tools
Site Actions
System Account
Home › New Web Part Page
A Web Part Page is a collection of Web Parts that combines list data, timely information, or useful graphics into a dynamic Web page. The layout and content of a Web Part Page can be set for all users and optionally personalized by each user.
I Like It
Tags & Notes
Home
BI Site
Pictures
Pictures
Libraries
Site Pages
Shared Documents
Data Connections
BCS Form Library
Request Forms
Retention Test
Invoices
Excel Workbooks
Track Changes
ListDefinitionProject1 - ListInstance1
ListDefinitionProject1 - ListInstance2
Lists
Calendar
Tasks
Custom List for IP
Name
Type a file name for your Web Part Page. The file name appears in headings and links throughout the site.
Name:
.aspx
Overwrite if file already exists?
Layout
Select a layout template to arrange Web Parts in zones on the page. Multiple Web Parts can be added to each zone. Specific zones allow Web Parts to be stacked in a horizontal or vertical direction, which is illustrated by differently colored Web Parts. If you do not add a Web Part to a zone, the zone collapses (unless it has a fixed width) and the other zones expand to fill unused space when you browse the Web Part Page.
Choose a Layout Template:
Header, Footer, 3 Columns
Full Page, Vertical
Header, Left Column, Body
Header, Right Column, Body
Header, Footer, 2 Columns, 4 Rows
Header, Footer, 4 Columns, Top Row
Left Column, Header, Footer, Top Row, 3 Columns
Right Column, Header, Footer, Top Row, 3 Columns
Save Location
Select the document library where you want the Web Part Page to be saved.
Document Library
Site Assets
Create
Cancel
Done
Trusted sites | Protected Mode: Off
100%
Start
2:08 PM
12/1/2010

#26

Setting the Home Page

While navigating through the pages in a site, you can select the Page tab in the ribbon bar to gain access to actions and properties for the page. One of those page actions is Make Homepage.

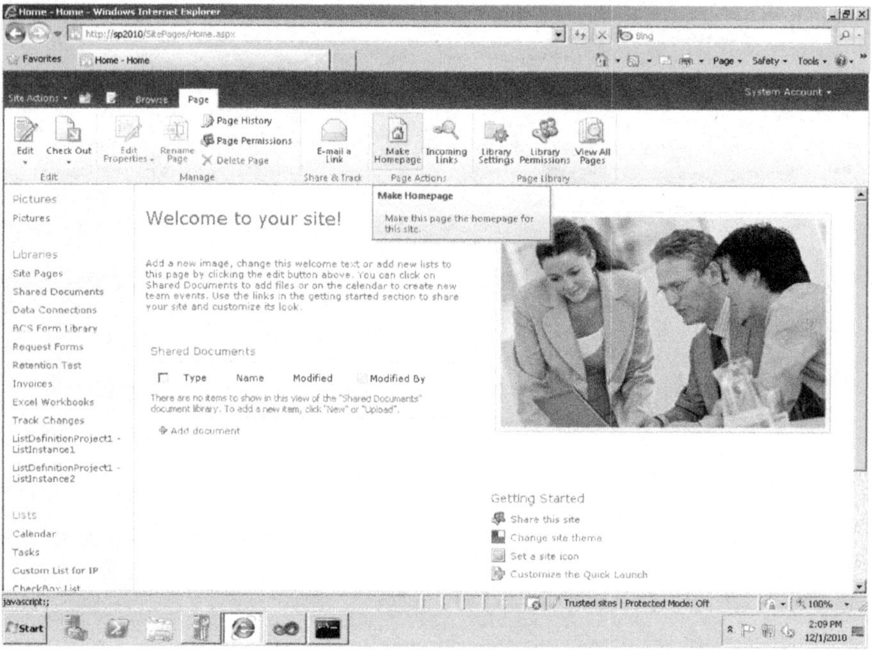

This will make the current page the home page. You get a confirmation/warning message before it happens.

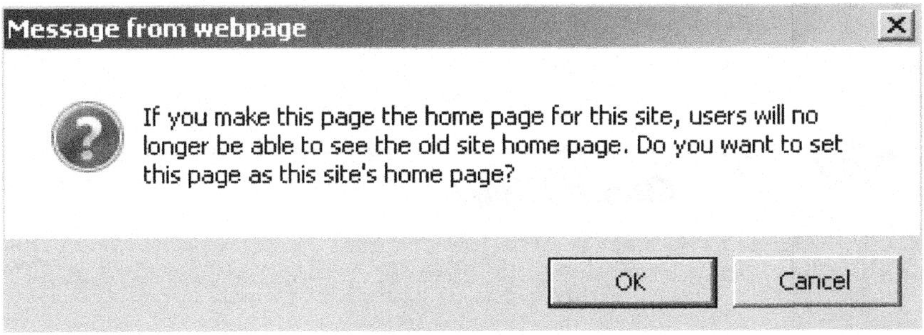

This message can be confusing. Some people may think that users will never be able to see the current home page ever again. It doesn't go away, it is just no longer the landing page for that site anymore – but it is still there.

#27

Quick Steps

While editing a list or library, you can customize the library ribbon by adding a Quick Step button. The button will be placed within the Items tab.

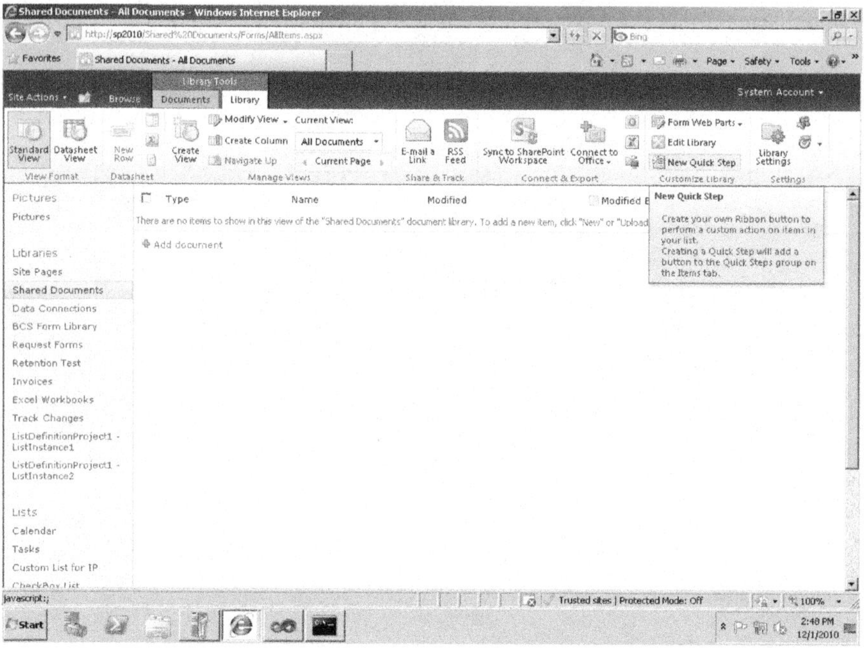

Although this sounds like you can perform various customized functions here, if you click om the New Quick Step button you will find out that you can only do two things – start a new workflow or start an existing workflow.

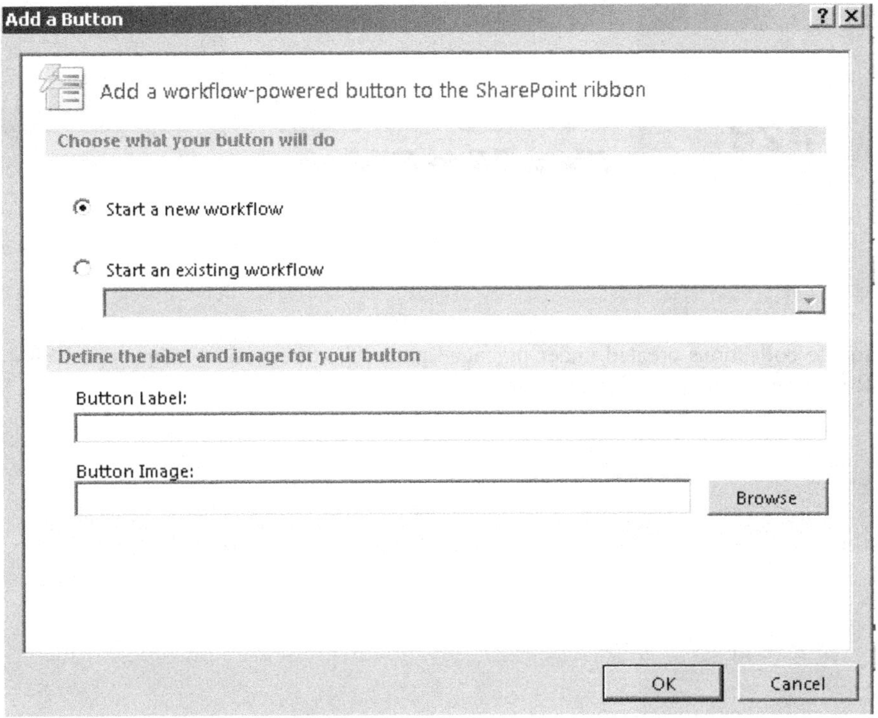

You can enter your own button label text and a nice icon for your Quick Step button. I am sure there will be other things that you can do eventually but for now your Quick Steps are programmed by creating workflows to perform the steps.

#28

Show/Hide Ribbon

In site collections created under managed paths, the Site Actions menu has a Show Ribbon or a Hide Ribbon menu item.

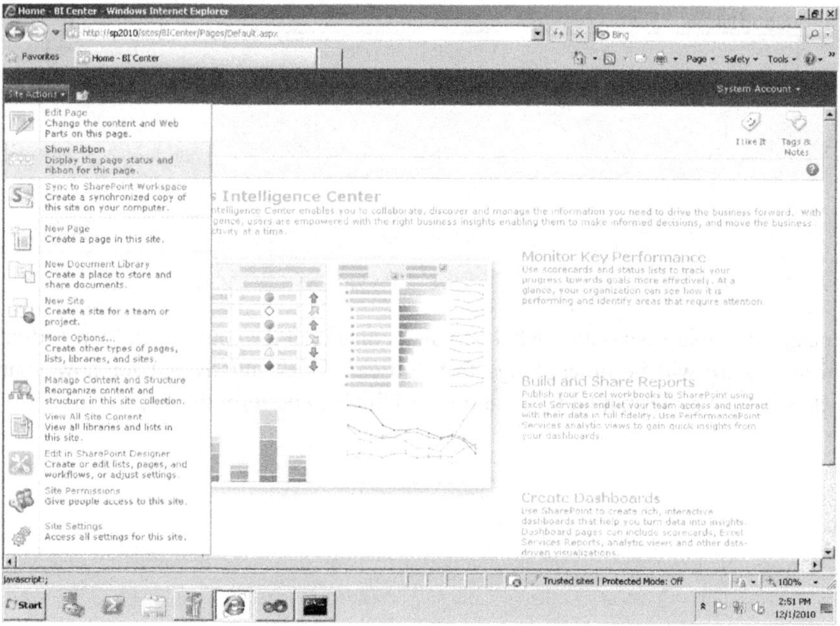

This appears toward the top of the menu list. If your page is not showing the top ribbon bar, you can make it appear by selecting the Show Ribbon from the Site Actions menu.

#29 Edit vs. Personalize Page

If you Edit the page you are changing it for everyone but on some site pages you can personalize the page. This option is available from the user menu on the right-hand side of the screen.

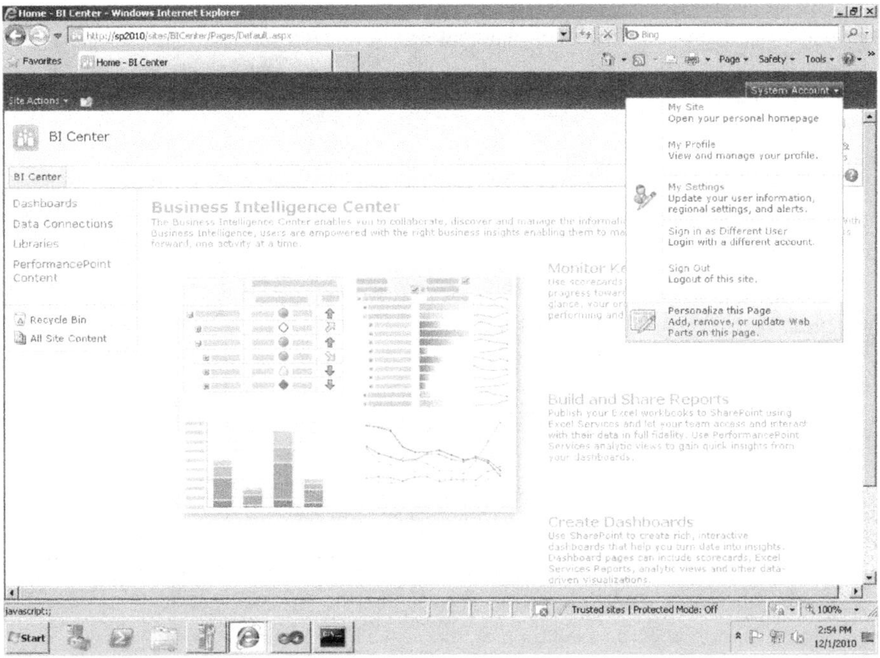

This generates a personal view that only you can see.

#30 Hide Ribbon Disabled

I had a scenario where the ribbon was showing but the Hide Ribbon menu item was disabled and there was no longer an Edit Page menu item.

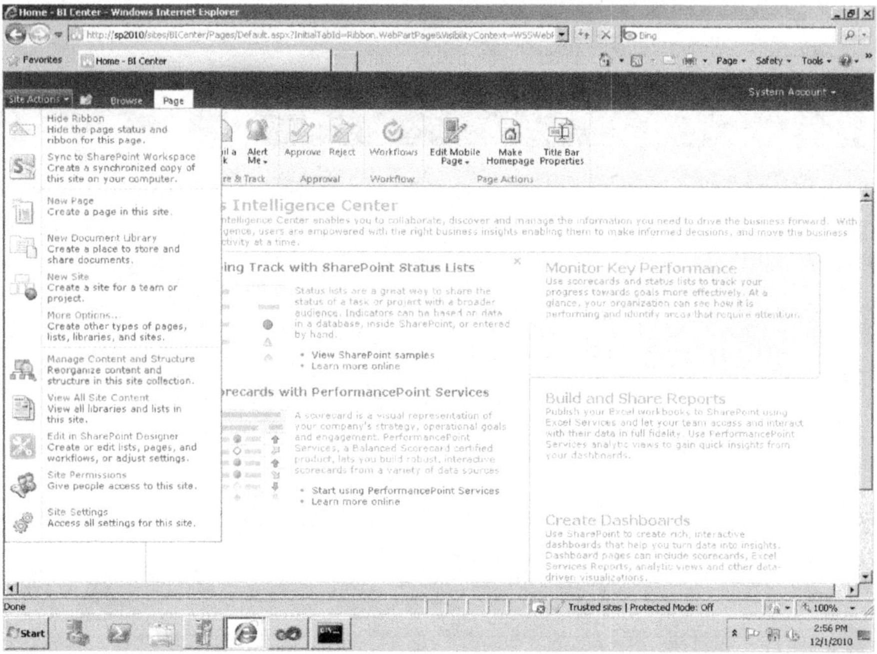

This happened during edits to the page along with personalizations to the page. What essentially causes this behavior is when you check out a page for editing. That will disable the Hide Ribbon menu item. If you switch to a personal view of the page while the page is checked out, the Edit Page option will not be shown on the Site Actions menu.

#31

GUIDs, GUIDS, GUIDs

This may be one of the things that people actually dislike. The SSP has been removed from MOSS 2007 but now each service application has its own set of databases and/or web services running under IIS.

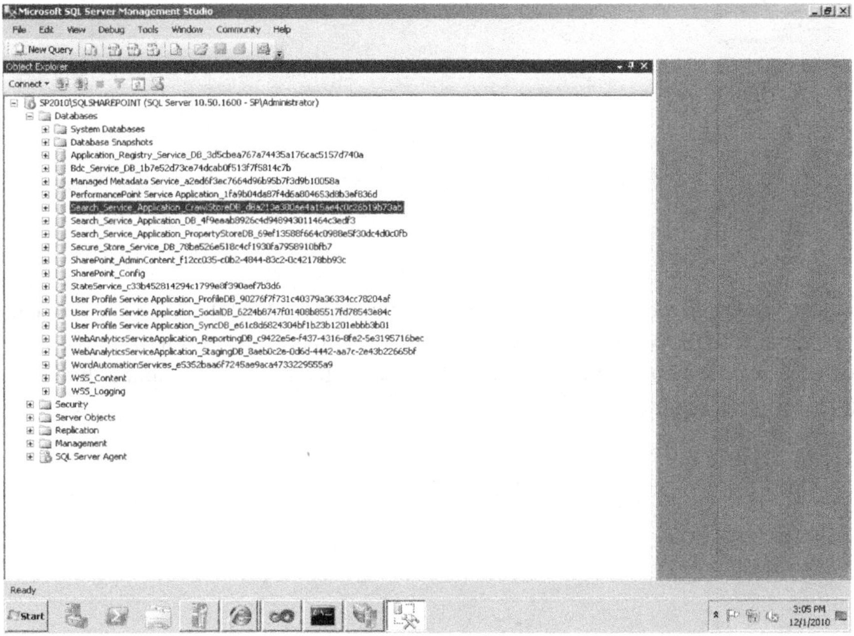

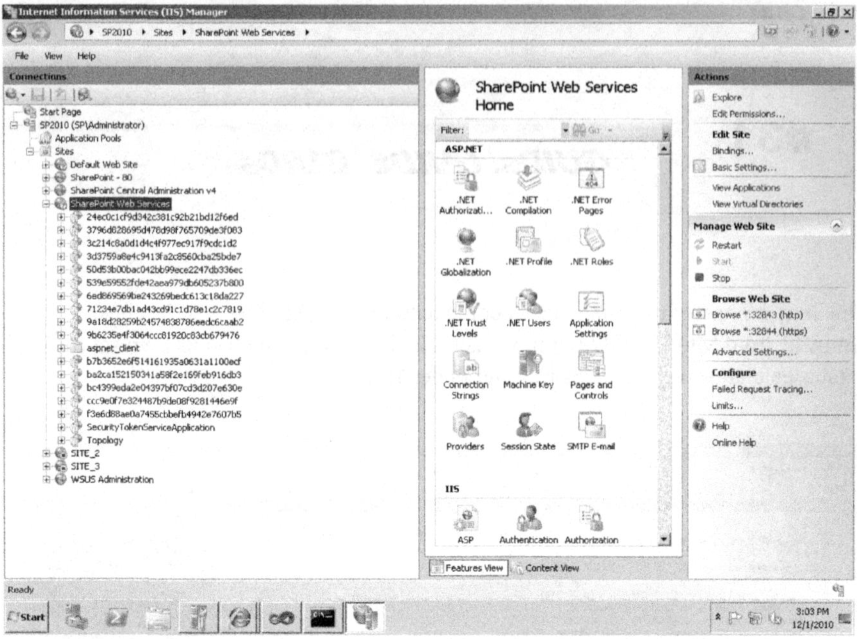

The databases and web services are either GUIDs or have GUIDs in their name. This is a big pain to DBAs and Administrators. However, there are several blogs out there that explain how to at least remove the GUIDs from the databases – although this varies by service application.

#32 Sign Out

You can use the user drop-down menu to Sign Out of the SharePoint Site.

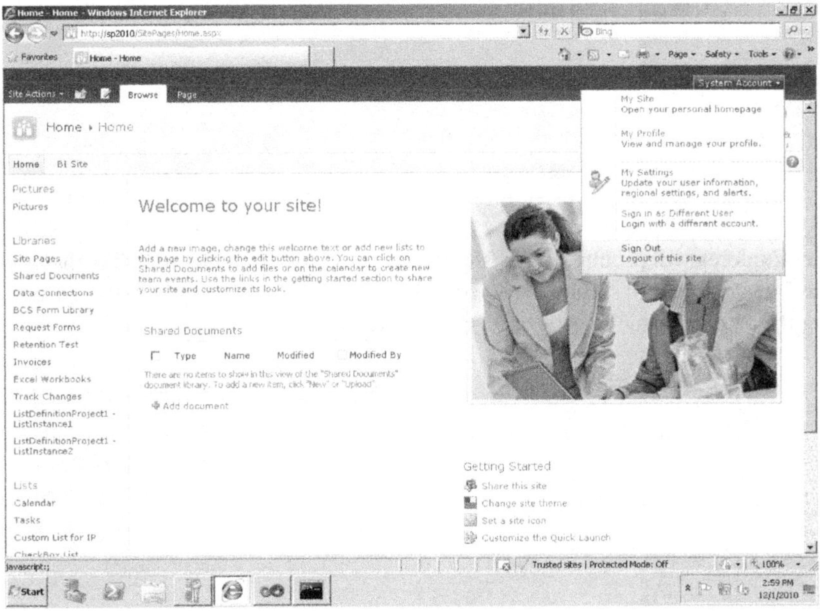

However, when in an intranet environment using windows authentication, this Sign Out doesn't really do anything. It is quicker just to close the browser as selecting Sign Out will force the browser to close anyway.

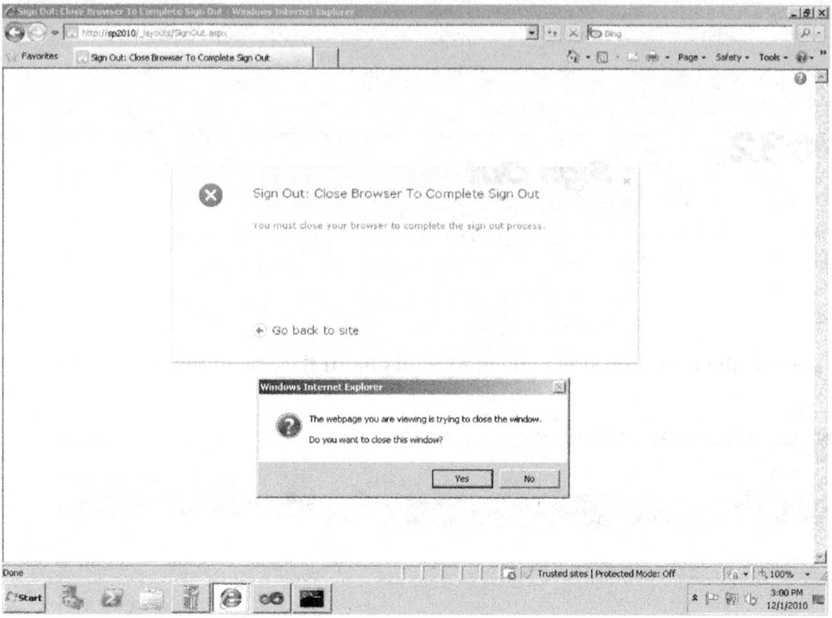

Internet Explorer will prompt you as shown above. If you click No and click the Go back to Site you are still signed in. So completing the sign out process in this case is closing the browser which you simply could have done in the first place.

#33

IIS Reset

There are many objects and assemblies that are cached within IIS and SharePoint. Therefore after deployments of these objects, a refresh of the IIS processes are needed (a.k.a. bouncing IIS).

Performing an iisreset will refresh the IIS processes and then hopefully your changes or modifications will work. This however causes users to experience a slight outage and many times you only need to recycle the application pool.

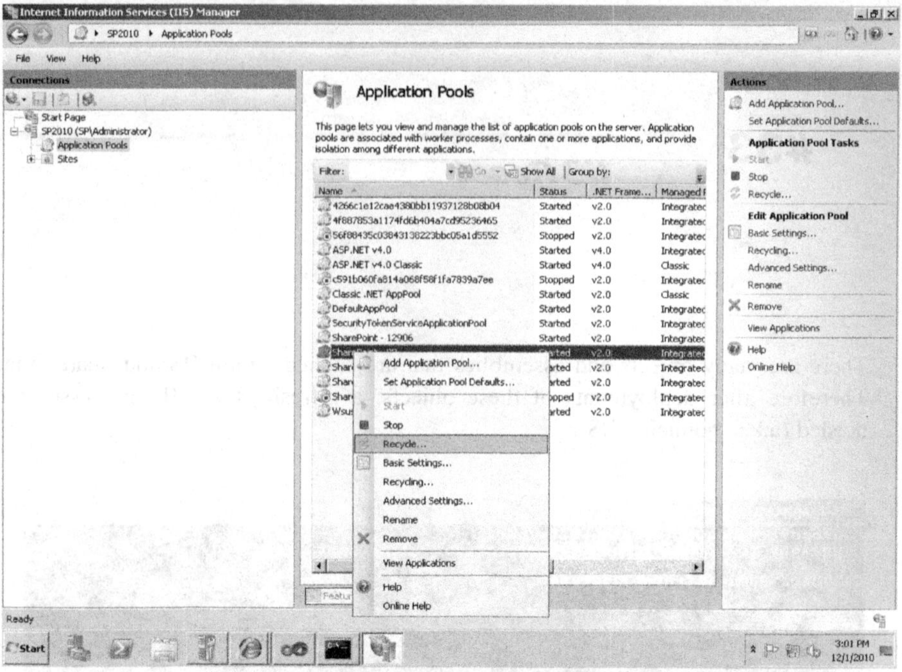

Most of the time, a full iisreset is not needed and you only need to recycle the app pool in IIS. This may cause a delay from a user perspective but it is not as disruptive as iisreset.

Some changes and modifications don't even require you to bounce IIS but when your changes do not work properly, there is always that question mark. If you recylce the app pool and your changes still don't work, is it your changes or do you need to do an iisreset?

One time I needed to resolve an issue on one particular web-front-end and finally just rebooting the server resolved all the issues. I spent hours trying to troubleshoot previously.

The good news is if you watch in Visual Studio 2010 as a solution is deployed, you'll see that the app pools are being recycled automatically (when applicable).

Conclusion

SharePoint is a huge product that provides all kinds of functionality to the enterprise. It is indeed hard to know everything and become an expert in all areas. An expert in SharePoint means that you have struggled through more areas than most and have learned what to do and what not to do. While this book wasn't designed to bestow this type of expertise, if you have at least learned a few things, then it was indeed worth your small investment.

Made in the USA
Monee, IL
04 November 2026

67382720R00030